SCALES

and

CHORDS

COMPLETE

A PROGRESSIVE APPROACH TO LEARNING MAJOR AND MINOR SCALES

WENDY MURPHY FACHINI

Authorunit
Number and Address
877-826-5888
17130 Van Buren Blvd., Ste. 238, Riverside, CA 92504

ISBN: 978-1-958895-95-5 (Paperback Edition)
ISBN: 978-1-958895-96-2 (E-book Edition)

Printed in the United States.

Contents

INTRODUCTION – HOW TO USE THIS BOOK

The purpose of this book is to provide a series of increasingly difficult scale, chord, and arpeggio exercises, creating a thorough background in Major, Harmonic Minor, and Chromatic Scales. Natural and Melodic minor scales, though not included in all of the exercises, may also be incorporated into music instruction. *Scales and Chords* is designed to be a supplement to any keyboard method of instruction, beginning about level 3 or Early Intermediate level. Most of the examples included in this book will not have fingerings included. The student should be familiar with whole steps, half steps, tetra chords, basic scale and chord fingerings, how to play chromatically, and I- IV- V chord progressions in some of the basic Major and Minor keys. I have included an appendices of scale and chord fingerings, 1 octave scales and I-IV-I-V-I chord progressions as a reference for all 12 major and minor scales.

Each level of instruction is rather involved. Beginning with Scale Pattern 1 the entire page of exercises is repeated in each key listed in the first exercise. Every time a level is completed, the student begins the next level's exercises back in the key of C Major. The new level is completed in each key listed in the first exercise. Beginning at Scale Pattern 5, the student will study the exercises for that level in all 12 major and 12 minor keys. It will take at least 24 weeks to complete each pattern thereafter. I have included a Keyboard Harmony level after Scale Pattern 6. This level gives a break from the general scale work and focuses on the chordal relationships between the keys around the Circle of Fifths

FOREWORD

When I began teaching piano back in 1994, I searched for a scale book to supplement my own instruction. As a young student, my teacher, Roberta Buck, gave me a thorough grounding in scales, chords, and arpeggios that I wished to pass on. What I found was a plethora of scale and chord reference books which, while useful, did not provide progressively more challenging exercises in scale or chord work. This was frustrating as I feel it is important to be comfortable executing scales, chords, and arpeggios. As a result, I began to write out the exercises remembered from my past and created this progressive scale and chords book.

For the past twenty five years, I have used this book in my studio, as a supplement to the various methods of instruction available to piano teachers today. It has proved to be an outstanding addition to my curriculum, producing many pianists that execute scales, chord progressions and arpeggios with ease. They understand that musical structure is built around scales and chords and leave my studio with a thorough grounding in these basic skills.

In this new complete edition, I have added scale fingerings and updated the wording on many of the exercises. I have also included material from Scales and Chords II to make a combined volume. Thank you to all my students for their input over the past 5 years. It has helped to make the instructions clearer and the book easier to use. Enjoy!

WHAT IS A MAJOR SCALE?

A major scale is a series of eight notes arranged in a pattern of whole steps and half steps. W W H W W W H, or C D E F G A B C where:

C to D = Whole Step

D to E = Whole Step

E to F = Half Step

F to G =Whole Step

G to A = Whole Step

A to B = Whole Step

B to C = Half Step.

WHAT IS A NATURAL MINOR SCALE?

A natural minor scale is a series of eight notes arranged in a pattern of whole steps and half steps. W H W W H W W, or A B C D E F G A where:

A to B = Whole Step

B to C = Half Step

C to D = Whole Step

D to E = Whole Step

E to F = Half Step

F to G = Whole step

G to A = Whole Step

Every Major Scale has a "relative" natural minor scale with the same key signature. The relative minor of any major scale, begins on the 6th tone of the major scale. You can also count three half steps down and two letter names down from the first note of the major scale. To create a harmonic minor scale, raise the 7th note of the natural minor scale by ½ step. Harmonic minors will be used in this book unless mentioned otherwise.

THE CIRCLE OF FIFTHS

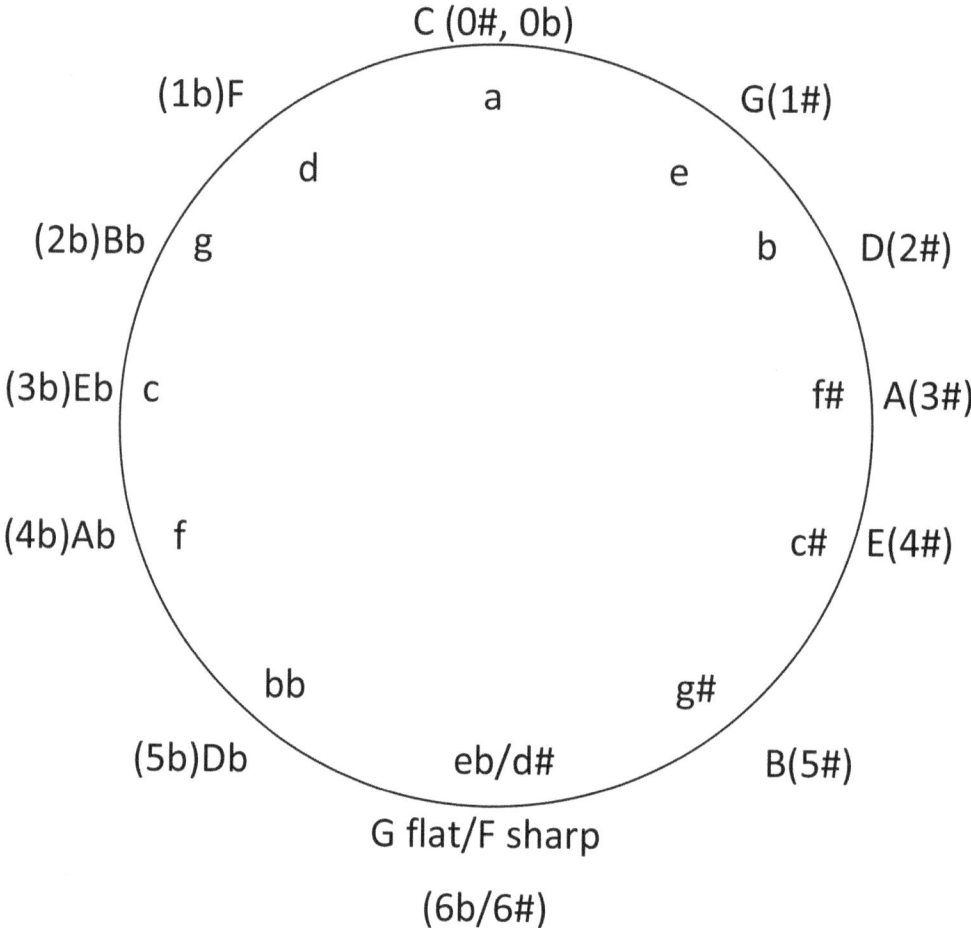

Moving up the keyboard by perfect 5ths beginning on C will take you around the circle of fifths clockwise adding a sharp to the key signature each time. Moving up the keyboard by perfect 4ths beginning on C will take you around the circle counterclockwise adding a flat to the key signature each time. MEMORIZE THIS!

Order of sharps: F C G D A E B

Order of flats: B E A D G C F

PREPARATORY SCALE PATTERN

Before studying major and minor scales, it is best to begin with 5 finger patterns in major and minor keys. The major 5 finger pattern is WWHW and has a "happy" sound. The minor 5 finger pattern is WHWW and has a "sad" sound.

5 Finger Positions

SCALE PATTERN 1

1. One octave Major scale hands separate.

C-G-D

Right Hand fingering is 1 2 3 1 2 3 4 5. Left Hand fingering is 5 4 3 2 1 3 2 1.

2. Build a triad on each note of the scale. Play hands separately. Major scale triads on each note of the scale:

Scale degree: I ii iii IV V vi vii I

Chord quality: M m m M M m dim. M

Left Hand fingering is 5 3 1. Right Hand fingering is 1 3 5.

3. Play the following pattern using the Major Scale Triads above. Play LH, RH, LH. RH.

Continue this pattern with all the triads up the scale

SCALE PATTERN 2

1. One octave scale, hands separate, then try together.

Major: C-G-D-A-E-F-B flat

Harmonic Minor: a-e-d

2. Play the following pattern building a triad from each note of the scale. Play LH, RH, LH, RH.

Continue this pattern with all the triads up the scale

M: I, ii, iii, IV, V, vi, vii/dim, I minor: i, ii/dim, iii/aug, iv, V, VI, vii/dim, i

3. Play the following pattern using inversions of the I chord.

Left Hand fingerings are 5 3 1, 5 3 1, 5 2 1

Right Hand fingerings are 1 3 5, 1 2 5, 1 3 5

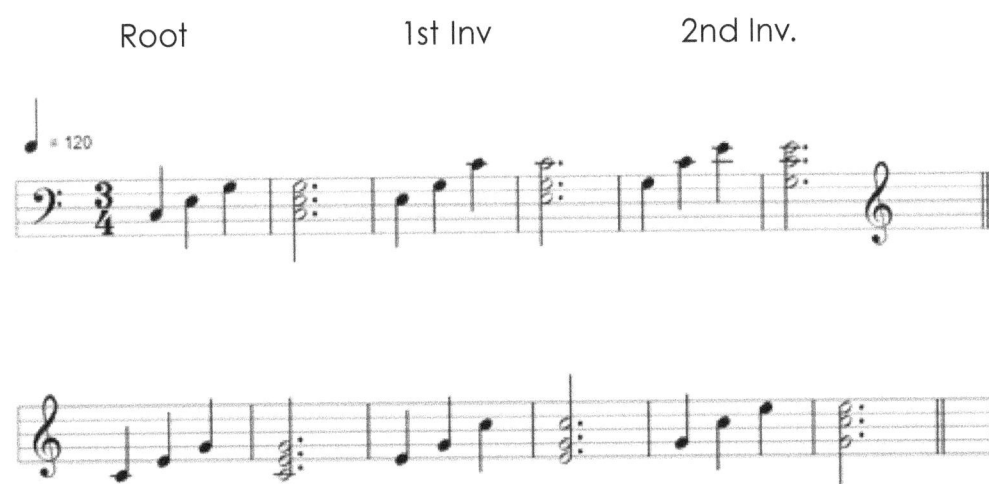

SCALE PATTERN 3

1. One octave scale, hands together.

   Major: **C-G-D-A-E-B-F-B flat-E flat-A flat**

   Harmonic Minor: a-e-d-b-g

2. Playing a Chromatic Scale (same every week)
   Chromatic Scales use all keys moving by half steps.
   Right Hand fingering begin on D: 1 3 1 2 3 1 3 1 3 1 2 3 1
   Left Hand fingering begin on D: 1 3 2 1 3 1 3 1 3 2 1 3 1

   Play hands alone, together parallel, and together contrary motion.

3. Chord Progressions

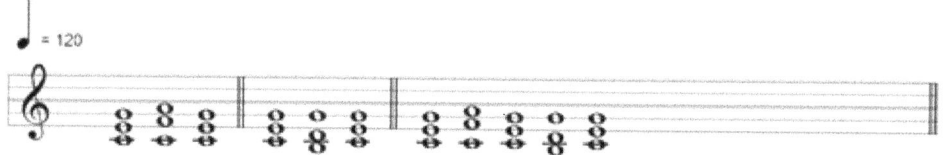

4. Chords up the scale: Hand over Hand. Play LH, RH, LH, RH. M: I,ii,iii,IV,V,vi,vii/dim,I minor: i,ii/dim,iii/aug,iv,V,VI,vii/dim,i

SCALE PATTERN 4

1. Two octave scale, hands together.

    Major: C-G-D-A-E-B-F-B flat-E flat-A flat-D flat-G flat

    Harmonic Minor: a-e-b-d-g-c-f

2. Play one octave scale in contrary motion. (optional)

3. Chords: hand over Hand up the scale as in level 3.

    Majors: I ii iii IV V vi vii/dim I
    Minors: i ii/dim iii/aug iv V VI vii/dim i

4. Chord progression I-IV-I-V-I with inversions. Hands separate, then together.

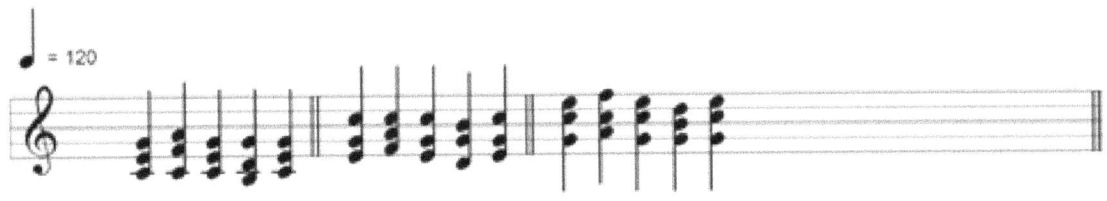

    Root position 1st inversion 2nd inversion

5. Chromatic Scale (see level 3) Play 2 octaves beginning on the key note (tonic) all weeks on this level. Play hands separate, together contrary motion, then together parallel motion.

SCALE PATTERN 5

1. Major and minor scales in rhythm, hands separately.

   Major: C-G-D-A-E-B-F-B flat-E flat-A flat-D flat-G flat

   Harmonic Minor: a-e-b-f sharp-c sharp-g sharp-e flat-b flat-f-c-g-d

   One octave –quarter notes

   Two octaves – eighth notes

   Three octaves – triplets

   Four octaves – sixteenth notes

2. Arpeggios- two octaves ascending and descending, hands separate. Line 1 Root position, Line 2 First Inversion, and Line 3 Second Inversion. See Appendix IV for two octave arpeggio basic fingerings.

   Root position: RH 1 2 3 1 2 3 5 3 2 1 3 2 1; LH 5 4 2 1 4 2 1 2 4 1 2 4 5

3. Chord Progression I-IV-I-V-I / i-iv-i-V-i no inversions, hands together.

4. Chromatic Scale – Four octaves, ascending and descending, beginning on the tonic of your current key, hands separate, try together.

SCALE PATTERN 6

1. All Major and Minor scales, 4 octaves hands together, ascending legato and descending staccato.
   Major: C-G-D-A-E-B-F-B flat-E flat-A flat-D flat-G flat
   Harmonic Minor: a-e-b-f sharp-c sharp-g sharp-e flat-b flat-f-c-g-d

2. All Major and minor arpeggios, 4 octaves hands separate, on I, IV, and V chord of each scale. Root position only, one hand at a time.

3. Chords, 4 octaves, run hand over hand.

   Majors: I – ii – iii – IV – V – vi – vii/dim - I

   Minors: i – ii/dim– iii/aug – iv – V – VI – vii/dim – i

4. Memorize order of sharps F-C-G-D-A-E-B
   Memorize order of flats B-E-A-D-G-C-F
   Memorize Circle of Fifths forward and backward:
   C-G-D-A-E-B-F sharp-D flat-A flat-E flat-B flat-F

KEYBOARD HARMONY

This level is all about learning Keyboard Mastery, or KM. KM is achieved when the pianist keeps his eyes entirely off the keyboard and on the music. Ideally, one should not need to look down at the keys to play. In these exercises, it is necessary to have memorized the circle of fifths, both in major and minor keys, forwards and backwards.

1. Warm up:

    Run hand over hand I chords chromatically and around the circle of fifths in Major and Minor keys. Week 1: Major keys,
    Week 2: Minor keys

2. Play the following pattern of broken and blocked chords in all keys.

    Week 1: Major keys, Week 2: Minor keys
    a. Chromatically
    b. Clockwise around the circle of fifths
    c. Counterclockwise around the circle of fifths

3. Run chords hand over hand around the circle of fifths using I-IV-V chord progression in each key. Week 1: Major keys, Week 2: minor keys For example, in C, major you would run a C chord, F chord, and G chord. Then moving to the key of G major, you would run a G chord, C chord, and D chord, continuing around the circle of fifths. (C-F-G, G-C-D, D-G-A etc.)

4. **I – IV – I – V – I** chord progression, chromatically in Major keys

5. **i – iv – i – V – i** chord progression, chromatically in Minor keys

SCALE PATTERN 7

1. All Major and Minor Scales, 4 octaves hands together, ascending pp-ff and descending ff-pp.
   Major: C-G-D-A-E-B-F-B flat-E flat-A flat-D flat-G flat
   Harmonic Minor: a-e-b-f sharp-c sharp-g sharp-e flat-b flat-f-c-g-d

2. All Major and Minor keys, 4 octave arpeggio ascending and descending where:
   a. Root position chord in LH, arpeggio in RH.
   b. First Inversion chord in RH, arpeggio in LH.

3. Extended Authentic Cadence (chord progression) M: I – IV – I – V – V7 – I m: i – iv – i – V – V7 - i

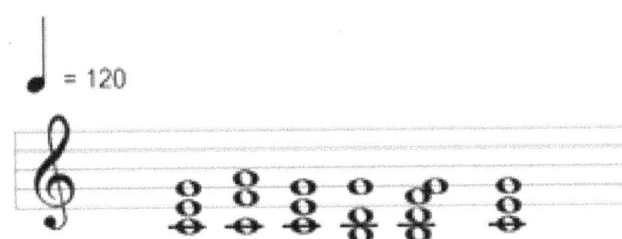

4. Chromatic Scale, hands separate, 2 octaves ascending, 1 octave descending. Do this 3 times, then descend to original starting note. Begin on the tonic note of your current key. Try hands together.

SCALE PATTERN 8

1. All Major and Minor scales, 2 octaves hands together, from the octave and in thirds (or tenths), in parallel and contrary motion.
    Major: C-G-D-A-E-B-F-B flat-E flat-A flat-D flat-G flat
    Harmonic Minor: a-e-b-f sharp-c-sharp-g sharp-e flat-b flat-f-c-g-d

2. Broken chord arpeggio, hands separate, pattern 1.
    a. RH fingering: 1-2-3-5, 1-2-4-5, 1-2-4-5, 1-2-3-5 and reverse for descending.
    b. LH fingering: 5-4-2-1, 5-4-2-1, 5-3-2-1, 5-4-2-1 and reverse for descending.

3. Chromatic Scale, one octave hands together, parallel and contrary motion from the octave and in thirds or tenths.

4. Octave study, hands separate.

5. Chord Progressions:

    Major: I – ii – vi – IV – ii – V - V7 – I
    Minor: i – ii/dim – VI – iv – ii/dim – V – V7 – i

SCALE PATTERN 9

1. All Major and Minor scales, 4 octaves hands together.
   Major: C-G-D-A-E-B-F-B flat-E flat-A flat-D flat-G flat
   Harmonic Minor: a-e-b-f sharp-c sharp-g sharp-e flat-b flat- f-c-g-d

2. Arpeggios and scales, 2 octaves hands separate.
   Ascend arpeggio, descend scale, ascend scale, descend arpeggio.

3. Arpeggios and chords, 2 octaves hands together.
   Root position chord LH, 2 octave arpeggio RH.
   First inversion chord RH, 2 octave arpeggio LH.

4. Arpeggios and chromatic, 2 octaves hands separate.
   Ascend. arpeggio, descend chromatic, ascend chromatic, descend arpeggio.

5. Broken chord arpeggio patterns, hands separate, ascending and descending.
   Patterns1, 2, 3, and 4. Use same fingering as in last level.
   Pattern 1 Pattern 2

Pattern 3 Pattern 4

6. Chord Progressions:

Major: I – IV – V7 – I   Minor: i – iv – V7 - i

       I – I/dim – V7 – I   i – i/dim – V7 - i

       I – V/dim – V7 – I   i – V/dim – V7 – i

       I – vi – ii – V7 – I   i – VI – ii/dim – V7– i

SCALE PATTERN 10

1. All Major and Minor scales, 4 octaves, hands together. Major: C-G-D-A-E-B-F-B flat-E flat-A flat-D flat-G flat

Harmonic Minor: a-e-b-f sharp-c sharp-g sharp-e flat-b flat-f-c-g-d

2. Arpeggios, hand over hand, through the chords of the scale.

Major: I – ii – iii – IV – V – vi – vii/dim – I
Minor: i – ii/dim – iii/aug – iv – V – VI – vii/dim – i

3. Maj/min 7th, Dim. 7th, Maj 6th, Aug. chord with passing tone. Play each, 2 octaves, hands separate, ascending and descending. RH 1234,12345 LH 54321,4321. Alter fingerings so 1st and 5th fingers are not on black keys.

4. Extended Authentic Cadence and inversions. I – IV – I – V – V7 – I Root position 1st Inversion 2nd Inversion

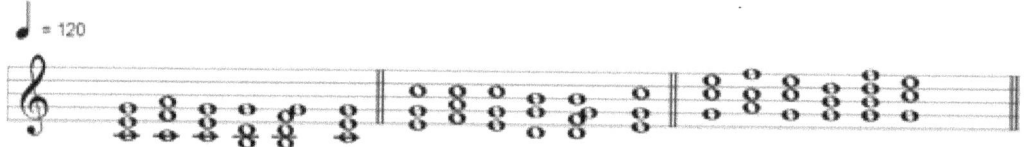

5. Chord Progressions: (minor progressions in parenthesis)

   Majors: I – V min – V – ii – V7 – I

           (i – V min – V – ii/dim – V7 – i)

           I – vi – IV – V7 – I (i – VI – iv – V7 – i)

           I – I/dim – V7 – I (i – i/dim – V7 – i)

           I – V/dim – V7 – I (i – V/dim – V7 – i)

14

SCALE PATTERN 11

1. All Major and Minor scales 2 octaves hands together. Do 2 times.
   a. LH staccato – RH legato
   b. LH legato – RH staccato
   Major: C-G-D-A-E-B-F-B flat-E flat-A flat-D flat-G flat
   Harmonic Minor: a-e-b-f sharp-c sharp-g sharp-e flat-b flat-f-c-g-d

2. Arpeggios, root position, hands separate, ascending and descending.
   a. 1 octave in quarter notes
   b. 2 octaves in eighth notes
   c. 3 octaves in triplets
   d. 4 octaves in sixteenth notes

3. Broken chord arpeggio patterns from level 9, ascending and descending inversions, hands together. Use the same fingering as level 9.
   Pattern 1 Pattern 2 Pattern 3 Pattern 4

4. Chromatic Scale, 2 octaves hands separate, as follows:
   Chromatic Scale ascending – Glissando descending
   Glissando ascending – Chromatic Scale descending

5. Chord Progression
   M: I–IV–I–V–I
   I–I/aug–I/dim–ii–IV–V7–I
   i-i7-IV-iv-i
   I–vi–ii–V7–I

   m: i-iv-i-V-i
   i-i/aug-i/dim-ii/dim-iv-V7-i I–I7–
   i-i7-IV-iv-i
   i-VI-ii/dim-V7-i

15

SCALE PATTERN 12

1. All Major and Minor scales, 4 octaves, hands together Major: C-G-D-A-E-B-F-B flat-E flat-A-flat-D flat-G flat
Harmonic Minor: a-e-b-f sharp-c sharp-g sharp-e flat-b flat-f-c-g-d

2. Broken chord arpeggios and inversions, ascending and descending, patterns 5 and
6. Use fingerings from patterns 1-4.

Broken Chord Arpeggios 5 and 6

3. Run chords up the scale, hand over hand. Make up a rhythm.
Major: I – ii – iii – IV – V – vi – vii/dim – I
Harmonic minor: i – ii/dim – iii/aug – iv – V – VI – vii/dim – i

4. Chord progression:
M: I – vi – ii – IV – V – V7 – I
m: i – VI – ii/dim – iv- V – V7 – i

5. Chromatic Scale, hands together four octaves staccato, beginning on the tonic of your key.

SCALE PATTERN 13

1. All major scales, four octaves ascending and descending, hands together.
   Major: C – G – D – A – E – B – F – B flat – E flat – A flat – D flat – G flat

2. All minor scales in natural, harmonic, and melodic form. Two octaves ascending and descending, hands together. Natural minor scales have the same key signature as their relative major scale. A harmonic minor scale raises the 7th note of the scale a half step. A melodic minor scale raises the 6th and 7th notes a half step ascending, and is a natural minor scale descending.
   Minor: a – e – b – f sharp – c sharp – g sharp – e flat – b flat – f – c - g - d

3. Dominant 7th (V7) chords and inversions. Hands alone. RH: 1245/1245/1235/1245
   LH: 5421/5421/5321/5421

4. Broken chord arpeggios and inversions, ascending and descending, patterns 7 and
   8. Use the same fingering as patterns 1-6.

Broken Chord Arpeggios 7 and 8

5. Chromatic Scale, hands together, 2 octaves contrary motion from the tonic.

SCALE PATTERN 14

1. All major and minor scales, four octaves hands together. Ascending: pp<ff /
   Descending ff>pp
   Major: C-G-D-A-E-B-F-B flat-E flat-A flat-D flat-G flat
   Harmonic Minor: a-e-b-f sharp-c sharp-g sharp-e flat-b flat f-c-g-d

2. Two octave arpeggios, hands together.
   a. Root position chord in LH/ 2 octave arpeggio in RH
   b. 2 octave arpeggio in LH / First inversion chord in RH

3. Fully diminished 7th chords and inversions, ascending and descending.

4. Sixth chords and inversions, ascending and descending.

5. Chord progressions in root, 1st inversion and 2nd inversion.
   Major: I – vi – ii – V7 – I
   Minor: i – VI – ii/dim – V7 – i

6. Chromatic Scales, two octaves ascending and descending, hands together
   in parallel thirds, with LH beginning on the tonic and RH a third above.

18

SCALE PATTERN 15

1. All major and minor scales, two octaves, hands together. Do twice.
   First time: Ascend scale/Descend arpeggio
   Second time: Ascend arpeggio/Descend scale
   Major: C-G-D-A-E-B-F-B flat-E flat-A flat D flat-G flat
   Harmonic Minor: a-e-b-f sharp-c sharp-g sharp-e-flat-b flat-f-c-g-d

2. Run arpeggios through the scale with chords, LH replaces RH.
   RH LH RH LH

   LH   RH   LH

3. Run the following chord progression on the tonic hands alone.
   M, m, dim, M, Aug, 6th, M7th, Mm7th, mm7th, dim7th, M

4. Chord Progressions
   I – I/dim – V7 – I i – i/dim – V7 – i
   I – V/dim – V7 – I i – V/dim – V7 – i

5. Chromatic Scale, two octaves hands together, in parallel 6ths. LH begins on
   the tonic and RH begins a 6th above.

SCALE PATTERN 16

1. All major and minor scales, two octaves hands together. Do twice.
   First time: Ascend scale/Descend chromatic
   Second time: Ascend chromatic/Descend scale
   Major: C-G-D-A-E-B-F-B flat-E flat-A flat-D flat-G flat
   Harmonic Minor: a-e-b-f sharp-c sharp-g sharp-e flat-b flat-f-c-g-d

2. Broken chord arpeggios in patterns 1, 2, 3, and 4. Hands together.

3. Chords up the scale, hands together, two octave arpeggio ascending and descending.

4. Chord progression
   M: I – iii – vi – IV – vii/dim – ii – V7 – I
   m: i – iii/aug – VI – iv – vii/dim – ii/dim – V7 – i

5. Chromatic Scale, hands together, on the octave, 1 note per hand.

SCALE PATTERN 17

1. All major and minor scales, two octaves hands together. Do twice.
   First time: LH staccato/RH legato
   Second time: LH legato/RH staccato
   Major: C-G-D-A-E-B-F-B flat-E flat-A flat-D flat-G flat
   Harmonic Minor: a-e-b-f sharp-c sharp-g sharp-e flat-b flat-f-c-g-d

2. Broken chord arpeggios in patterns 5, 6, 7, and 8. Hands together.

   Pattern 5 Pattern 6 Pattern 7 Pattern 8

3. Chord progression
   M: I – I/aug – I/dim – vi – ii – IV – V7 – I
   m: i – i/aug – i/dim – VI – ii/dim – iv – V7 – i

4. Chromatic Scale, three octaves hands together, contrary motion from the tonic.

SCALE PATTERN 18

1. All major and minor scales in the following Grand Scale pattern. Major: C-G-D-A-E-B-F-B flat-E flat-A flat-D flat-G flat
   Harmonic Minor: a-e-b-f sharp-c sharp-g sharp-e flat-b flat-f-c-g-d

2. Broken chord arpeggios patterns 1-8, hands together.
   Pattern 1 Pattern 2 Pattern 3 Pattern 4

Pattern 5 Pattern 6 Pattern 7 Pattern 8

3. Chord progression
   M: I – v/minor – iii – vi – ii – V7 – I
   m: i – v/minor – iii/aug – VI – ii/dim – V7 – i

4. Chromatic Scale, hands together, in the Grand Scale pattern above.

22

APPENDIX I – ONE OCTAVE SCALE FINGERINGS

Major Scales

C: RH - 123 12345/54321 321
      C D E F G A B C
    LH - 54321 321/123 12345

G: RH – 123 12345/54321 321
      G A B C D E F# G
    LH – 54321 321/123 12345

D: RH – 123 12345/54321 321
      D E F# G A B C#D
    LH – 54321 321/123 12345

A: RH – 123 12345/54321 321
      A B C# D E F# G# A
    LH – 54321 321/123 12345

E: RH – 123 12345/54321 321
      E F# G# A B C# D# E
    LH – 54321 321/123/12345

B: RH – 123 12345/54321 321
      B C# D# E F# G# A# B
    LH – 4321 4321/1234 1234

F: RH – 1234 1234/4321 4321
      F G A Bb C D E F
    LH – 54321 321/123 12345

Bb: RH – 4 123 1234/4321 321 4
      Bb C D Eb F G A Bb
    LH – 321 4321 3/3 1234 123

Eb: RH – 3 1234 123/321 4321 3
      Eb F G Ab Bb C D Eb
    LH – 321 4321 3/3 1234 123

Ab: RH – 34 123 123/321 321 43
      Ab Bb C Db Eb F G Ab
    LH – 321 4321 3/3 1234 123

Harmonic Minor Scales

Cm: RH – 123 12345/54321 321
      C D Eb F G Ab B C
    LH - 54321 321/123 12345

Gm: RH – 123 12345/54321 321
      G A Bb C D Eb F# G
    LH – 54321 321/123 12345

Dm: RH – 123 12345/54321 321
      D E F G A Bb C# D
    LH – 54321 321/123 12345

Am: RH – 123 12345/54321 321
      A B C D E F G# A
    LH – 54321 321/123 12345

Em:RH – 123 12345/54321 321
      E F# G A B C D# E
    LH – 54321 321/123/12345

Bm: RH – 123 12345/54321 321
      B C# D E F# G A# B
    LH – 4321 4321/1234 1234

Fm: RH – 1234 1234/4321 4321
      F G Ab Bb C Db E F
    LH – 54321 321/123 12345

Bbm: RH – 4 123 1234/4321 321 4
      Bb C Db Eb F Gb A Bb7
    LH – 21 321 432/234 123 12

Ebm: RH – 3 1234 123/321 4321 3
      Eb F Gb Ab Bb Cb D Eb
  21 4321 32/23 1234 12

G#m: RH - 34 123 123/321 321 43
      G# A# B C# D# E Fx G#
    LH – 321 4321 3/3 1234 123

Major Scales

Db: RH – 23 1234 12/21 4321 32
Db Eb F Gb Ab Bb C Db
LH – 321 4321 3/3 1234 123

Gb: RH – 234 123 12/21 321 432
Gb Ab Bb Cb Db Eb F Gb
LH – 4321 321 4/4 123 1234

Harmonic Minor Scales

C#m: RH – 34 123 123/321 321 43
C# D# E F# G# A B# C#
LH – 321 4321 3/3 1234 123

F#m: RH – 34 123 123/321 321 43
F# G# A B C# D E# F#
4321 321 4/4 123 1234

Fingering Tips:

1. Group same fingerings together. CGDAE major and minor scales have the same fingerings.

2. Know where the 4th finger plays in each hand for each scale.

3. Find where the same finger plays together on both hands/same note.

4. Flat Key fingering rules: RH 4th finger always plays on Bb. LH 4th finger always plays on the new flat, in the Major keys starting with Eb.

APPENDIX II – CHORD PROGRESSIONS

I-IV-I-V-I chord progression fingering:

RH – Root position: 135, 135, 135, 125, and 135

    First inversion: 125, 135, 125, 135, and 125

    Second inversion: 135, 125, 135, 135, and 135

LH – Root position: 531, 521, 531, 531, and 531

    First inversion: 531, 531, 531, 521, and 531

    Second inversion: 521, 531, 521, 531, and 521

APPENDIX III - CHROMATIC SCALES

Fingering tips:

1. The 3rd finger in each hand will play all the black keys.

2. The thumb will play all the white keys except where two white keys are adjoining. The fingering is then 1-2 or 2-1 depending on which hand is playing. At no time should fingers 1 and 2 cross each other.

3. RH 2nd finger always plays on F and C
    LH 2nd finger always plays on E and B

APPENDIX IV - 2 OCTAVE ARPEGGIOS
BASIC FINGERING

RH - Root position: 1-2-3-1-2-3-5-3-2-1-3-2-1

    1st inversion: 1-2-4-1-2-4-5-4-2-1-4-2-1

    2nd inversion: 1-2-4-1-2-4-5-4-2-1-4-2-1

LH – Root position: 5-4-2-1-4-2-1-2-4-1-2-4-5

    1st inversion: 5-4-2-1-4-2-1-2-4-1-2-4-5

    2nd inversion: 5-3-2-1-3-2-1-2-3-1-2-3-5

The thumb does not play on the black keys. Alter fingerings to accommodate.

APPENDIX V – SCALE DEGREE NAMES

Major: I – ii – iii – IV – V – vi – vii/dim – I

Minor: i – ii/dim – iii/aug – iv – V – VI – vii/dim – i

First scale note = Tonic, tonal center, key name

Second scale note = Supertonic, a whole step above the tonic

Third scale note = Mediant, midway between the tonic and dominant

Fourth scale note = Subdominant, a perfect fifth lower than the tonic

Fifth scale note = Dominant, a perfect fifth higher than the tonic

Sixth scale note = Submediant, midway between the subdominant and tonic

Seventh scale note = Leading tone, leads melodically up to the tonic

APPENDIX VI – ADDITIONAL CHORD PROGRESSIONS

M: I – vi – vi7 – ii7 – V7 – I

M: I – iii– vi7 – ii7 – V7 – I

M: I – vi – IV – V/aug – V7 – I

M: I – ii7 – V7 – vi7 – IV – V7 – I

m: i – VI – VI7 – ii/dim7 – V7 – i

m: i – iii/aug – VI7 – ii/dim7 – V7

– i m: i – VI – iv – V/aug – V7 – i

m: i – ii/dim7 – V7 – VI7 – iv –V7 – i

APPENDIX VII – BROKEN ARPEGGIO
PATTERNS 9, 10, 11, 12

APPENDIX VIII – MAJOR AND HARMONIC MINOR SCALES

Major and Minor Scales

Major and Minor Scales

Major and Minor Scales

www.ingramcontent.com/pod-product-compliance
Lightning Source LLC
Chambersburg PA
CBHW041524120626

46551CB00018B/2568